APPLE WATCH SERIES 6

A Complete Step By Step User Guide For Beginners And Seniors To Learn How To Use The Apple Watch Series 6 Like A Pro With The Aid Of Pictures

BY

HERBERT A. CLARK

Table of Contents

INTRODUCTION 1

WHAT'S NEW IN WATCHOS 7 2

HOW TO SET UP YOUR WATCH 11

SET UP FOR FAMILY MEMBER...........21

HOW TO USE THE APPLE WATCH 33

HOW TO CHANGE THE APPLE WATCH BAND 37

Solo loop 40

Milanese loop..41

Link bracelet 42

WATCH FACE 46

Change the watch face on Apple Watch.... 46

Customize the watch face on Apple Watch 46

Add more information to your watch face 49

Create a new copy of the watch face 50

Remove watch face from Apple Watch......51

Change the time displayed on Apple Watch 52

Hide now playing on Apple Watch 53

WORKOUT APP 55

Begin a workout 55

Workout management 56

Add workout 57

Workout reminders 58

Record workout 59

Workout settings 60

ACTIVITY APP 62

View activity on Apple Watch 62

View activity log 63

View activity trends 64

View workout history 65

View awards 66

Share activity data 66

Begin a competition 68

Compare activity data on Apple Watch 68

Compare activity data on iPhone 69

Complete the competition 69

PHONE APP 70

Answer the call 70

During a call 71

Listen to voicemail 73

Make phone calls on apple watch 74

Make a call 74

Input a phone number on your Apple 75

Make calls over Wi-Fi 76

SLEEP APP 78

Set up sleep mode 78

Adjust your sleep schedule 85

Disable your sleep schedule 89

NOISE APP 91

Set up the noise application 92

Get noise alert 92

View information about ambient sound
levels 93

Turn off noise measurement 93

MEMOJI APP 94

Create a Memoji 94

Edit Memoji is present 97

Duplicate Memoji 97

Delete Memoji 99

Create a Memoji watch face 100

Use Memoji in Messages on Apple Watch
.... 102

HANDWASHING FEATURE............... 103

Apple Watch that supports hand washing
.... 103

How to enable watchOS 7 handwash
detection 104

Test Handwashing detection on Apple
Watch.. 106

How to check hand washing data in Health
app on iPhone... 106

HEART RATE APP 108

View your heart rate 108

Monitor your heart rate during a workout
.... 109

View a graph of heart rate data............... 110

Activate heart rate data........................... 110

Receive notifications about high or low
heart rate 111

Receive notifications about irregular heart
rhythms... 112

CYCLE TRACKING 114

Set up your monthly cycle data in the
Health application on iPhone 114

Customize cycle tracking options in Health app on iPhone 118

Register a period for cycle tracking in the Health app on iPhone 122

Record period on Apple watch 124

Record a cycle symptom in Apple Watch 125

Delete Cycle Tracking Data in Health App on iPhone 126

Delete the cycle tracker app 129

SIRI 131

Set up Siri on Apple Watch 131

Activate Siri on Apple Watch 132

Apple Watch Siri Commands 133

Add Siri to the face of your Apple Watch .134

BREATHE 136

COMPASS 139

MEASURE BLOOD OXYGEN LEVEL WITH APPLE WATCH 142

How the Apple Watch measures oxygen levels 142

Measure blood oxygen with Apple Watch145

ECG 148

Set up the Apple Watch ECG app 149

Take an ECG on Apple Watch................. 149

Meaning of Apple Watch ECG results 151

Sharing your ECG result........................152

FALL DETECTION 153

How to activate fall detection 154

Making an emergency call after a fall 156

Adding friends and family to your emergency contact list 157

Settings to be enabled for fall detection to work.. 158

How to disable fall detection 158

APPLE PAY... 160

Set up and add cards to Apple Pay 160

Making use of Apple Pay on Apple Watch 162

TIPS AND TRICKS 164

Wake up to the last application used...... 164

Enlarge the text on the screen 165

Silence alerts with the palm of your hand165

Hide clock apps.................................... 166

Find an iPhone using your watch 167

Quick access to Zoom and VoiceOver..... 168

Take a screenshot 169

Force restart Apple Watch 169

Set your watch in just five minutes 169

Turn off the snooze of your alarms 170

Create custom message responses in advance 171

Always send your text as voice 172

Place a call on hold until you find your iPhone 172

Turn on Walkie-Talkie 173

Clear all notifications with Force Touch ..173

Mark emails with Force Touch 174

Choose which mailboxes will appear on your watch 174

Switch between day and List views on the calendar 175

Build your leaving time in the calendar alerts 175

Put the watch on a power backup 176

Unlock your Mac with Apple Watch 176

Customize the application dock 177

Take out the water after swimming 177

Use theater mode 178

Listen to music 179

Listen to podcasts 180

Talk to someone with Walkie-Talkie 181

INTRODUCTION

In the five years since it was launched, the Apple Watch has evolved from the series first model that we first saw in 2015 to the golden standard for modern smartwatches. The just-announced Series 6 continues down this path. The Series 6 features the most watch colors in product history, including blue, (PRODUCT) RED, graphite, and gold. It also contains the device's first blood oxygen sensor feature, a feature that has become a standard in the smartwatch market and was highly anticipated by Apple fans. Apple Watch Series 6 also features fast app animation and a flexible interface, due in particular to the new A14 processor and Apple's sleek new WatchOS7. The new watch faces bring a more artistic look to your smartwatch.

WHAT'S NEW IN WATCHOS 7

Personalize and share your watch face:
Create a watch face using your favorite
complications (even multiple complications
from the same app) and share them via text
message, email, or online link.

The Apple Watch screen displays a watch face
share message with the recipient's name at the
top, the watch face-name below, and a
message below that says "Check this watch
face."

Manage Your Sleep: Apple Watch with watchOS 7 can help you reach your sleep goals. Just set a bedtime schedule and then go to bed. When you wake up, see how long you've slept and check the direction of your sleep over the past two weeks.

The sleep screen shows the night's sleep schedule. Bedtime near the summit is set at 11:00 p.m. Below is the time to wake up at 7 AM.

Countdown to Clean: With watchOS 7, Apple Watch can detect when to start washing your hands and encourage you to stay within the time recommended by global health organizations.

Manage a relative's watch: kids, and also grown-ups, can benefit from making use of an Apple Watch. With watchOS 7, you can set up and manage a Watch for your kid, or anybody in your Family Sharing group.

How do you say ...: stuck on a word or phrase in another language? Siri can now translate a lot of languages, straight from Apple Watch.

Get moving in new ways: Open the Workout app and start one of four new exercises: dance, functional strength training, core training, or cool down. View exercise results in the Fitness app on iPhone.

Bike directions: with watchOS 7, Apple Watch gives bike directions, with maps that show changes in bike lanes, altitude, and congested roads.

The Maps screen displays an overview of cycling directions, including changes in altitude, estimated travel time, and distance.

Choose a shortcut: with one click, now you can use the shortcuts you created on iPhone and even add them as watch face complications.

More alternatives to safeguard your hearing: Apple Watch does not only warn you of exposure to loud sounds surrounding you, it also reduces loud sounds played through headphones automatically.

The noise display shows a decibel level of 100 dB. Below is a warning for prolonged exposure to sounds at this level.

New watch face: watchOS 7 presents new watch faces: Stripes, Typograph, Count Up, Chronograph Pro, Artist, GMT, and Memoji. Add color filters to any watch face in the photo app.

Not all features are available in all regions and on all models.

HOW TO SET UP YOUR WATCH

BEFORE YOU START

To set up and use Apple Watch, you need an iPhone with the latest version of iOS. You also need to make sure that Bluetooth is turned on on your iPhone and that it is connected to Wi-Fi or cellular network.

If you have already set up an Apple Watch but want to use it with a different iPhone, you can transfer your Apple Watch and its contents to your new iPhone.

TURN YOUR APPLE WATCH ON AND TURN IT ON

To switch on your Watch, long-press the side button till you see the Apple logo. This might take a few seconds.

PLACE YOUR WATCH NEAR YOUR IPHONE

Wait for the message "Use your iPhone to set up the Apple Watch" on your iPhone, then click "Continue." If you do not get this message, launch the Watch application on your Phone, touch All Watches, and afterward touch Pair New Watch.

If this is your Apple Watch, tap Set up for me. Or tap Set a family member, then follow the steps to set the watch for a member of your family.

HOLD YOUR IPHONE OVER THE ANIMATION

Center the watch face in the viewfinder of your iPhone. Wait for a message that your Apple Watch is paired.

If you can't use the camera, tap Manually pair your Apple Watch, then follow the steps that appear.

SET UP AS NEW OR RESTORE FROM BACKUP

If you are using the apple watch for the first time, touch Set Up as New Apple Watch. If not, touch Restore from Backup. If prompted, update your Apple Watch to the latest watchOS version.

Read the terms and conditions and click Accept, then click Accept again to continue.

SIGN IN WITH YOUR APPLE ID

If prompted, enter your Apple ID password. If not inquired, you can log in later from the Watch app: touch General> Apple ID, then sign in. Some features that require a mobile phone number won't work on Apple Watch cellular models unless you're signed in. To iCloud.

If **Find My** is not set up on your iPhone, you will be prompted to turn on Activation Lock. If you see the Activation Lock screen, your Apple Watch is already associated with an Apple ID. You must enter the email address and password for this Apple ID to proceed with setup. If your Apple Watch was previously owned by someone else, you may have to contact the previous owner to help remove the Activation Lock.

CHOOSE YOUR SETTINGS

Apple Watch shows you the settings that you share with your iPhone. If you turn on features like Find My, Location Services, Wi-Fi Calling, and Diagnostics for your iPhone, these settings will automatically turn on for your Apple Watch.

You can then choose to use other settings, such as route tracking and Siri. If Siri hasn't been set up on your iPhone yet, it will turn on after you select this option. You can also choose the text size on your watch.

CREATE A PASSWORD

You can decide to skip creating a password, but you may need one for features such as Apple Pay.

On an iPhone, tap Create Passcode or Add Long Passcode, then switch to Apple Watch to enter the new passcode. To skip, tap Don't add a password.

CHOOSE FEATURES AND APPS

After that, you will also be required to set up Apple Pay by adding a card. Next, we'll walk you through setting up features like watchOS and SOS updates, and automatic activity. On Apple Watch cellular models, you can also configure the cellular network.

Lastly, you can install your applications that are supported by Apple Watch or decide to install the applications later.

WAIT FOR YOUR DEVICES TO SYNC

Determined by the amount of info you have, the sync may take time. While waiting for your watch to sync, try Apple Watch basics to learn a little bit about how to wear your watch.

Hold your devices together until you hear it ring and feel the gentle touch of your Apple Watch, then push the Digital Crown.

Start making use of your Apple Watch

SET UP FOR FAMILY MEMBER

WatchOS 7 Family Settings permits family members who do not own an iPhone to enjoy the benefits and features of Apple Watch.

HOW IT WORKS

With Family Setup, your family members who don't have their iPhone can use the Apple Watch to do things like make phone calls, send messages, and share their location with you.

After setting a watch for a family member, you can use your iPhone to manage some of the watch's capabilities.

Keep in mind that some Apple Watch features depend on the iPhone and are not accessible on the Apple Watch that pairs with Family Settings.

WHAT DO YOU NEED

1) Apple Watch Series 4 or later with cellular or Apple Watch SE with cellular, with watchOS 7 or later
2) iPhone 6s or later with iOS 14 or later for the initial watch setup
3) An Apple ID for you and the other person who will be using your Apple Watch
4) Family Sharing setting that includes the individual who will make use of the Apple Watch

No cellular plan is needed to set up a Watch for a family member, but it is needed for some features.

PUT ON YOUR WATCH AND TURN IT ON

If your Apple Watch isn't new, erase it first.

Then wear the watch or have family members wear it. Long press the side button until the Apple logo is displayed on your watch screen.

KEEP THE WATCH CLOSE TO YOUR IPHONE

Hold your Apple Watch close to your iPhone. Wait for the phrase "Use your iPhone to set up the Apple Watch" on your iPhone, then click "Continue." If you don't see this message, launch the Watch application on your iPhone, click on All Watches, then click on Pair New Watch.

Touch a set up for a family member, and then touch Continue on the next screen.

PAIR THE WATCH WITH YOUR IPHONE

Hold your iPhone over the clock animation. Center the watch face on your iPhone's viewfinder, then wait for a message to appear that your Apple Watch is paired. If you can't use the camera, tap Manually pair your Apple Watch, then follow the steps that appear.

Then, tap Set Up Apple Watch.

SET A PASSWORD

Touch Accept on the Terms and Conditions screen, then choose a text size for Apple Watch.

After that, set a password to keep the watch safe.

CHOOSE A FAMILY MEMBER

Pick the family member who would make use of the Apple Watch. If they don't appear, tap Add a new family member.

Input the family member's Apple ID passcode, afterward tap on Next.

ACTIVATE ASK TO BUY

Turn on Ask to Buy if you want to approve downloads or purchases made on your Apple Watch.

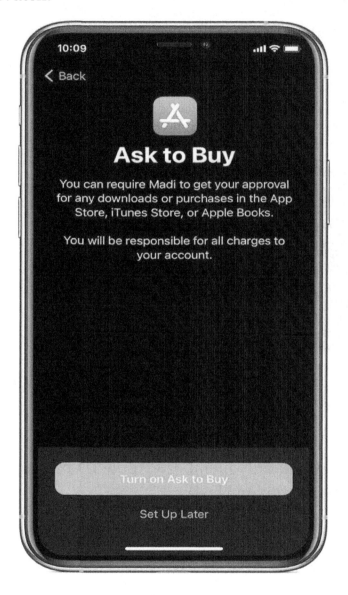

SET UP WI-FI AND MOBILE DATA

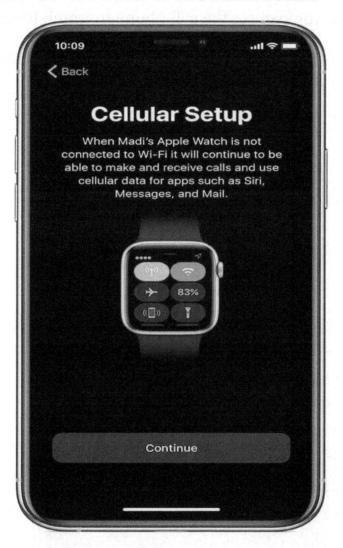

If your iPhone cell phone provider supports family settings, you can add the watch to your plan. If your carrier doesn't support it, you might be able to use an alternate operator. Then you can set the cell phone to watch later.

Next, choose whether you want to share the current Wi-Fi network with Apple Watch.

ACTIVATE OTHER FEATURES

On the following screens, choose whether you want to activate and configure additional Apple Watch features. This includes location services for Find People, Siri, Apple Cash Family, iCloud messages, health data, SOS emergencies, emergency contacts, medical ID, activity, training path tracking, and photos.

SET UP SHARED CONTACTS AND SCHOOLTIME

After that, you will be asked to set up the contacts that will be available on the Apple Watch. Update the contact information of your family members then make sure their contact card is updated as well.

You can then choose trusted people from your Contacts app to share them on Apple Watch. You can manage these shared contacts later and set restrictions on device usage time on your iPhone.

Finally, set a screen time passcode for the watch and run Schooltime. When done, click OK to start using your Apple Watch.

HOW TO USE THE APPLE WATCH

PUSH OR TURN THE DIGITAL CROWN

- Press to display the watch screen or the home screen.
- Double click to return to the last application.
- Press and hold to use Siri.
- Rotate to zoom in, pan, or adjust what appears on the screen
- On Apple Watch Series 2 or later and Apple Watch SE, rotate to unlock the screen while swimming.

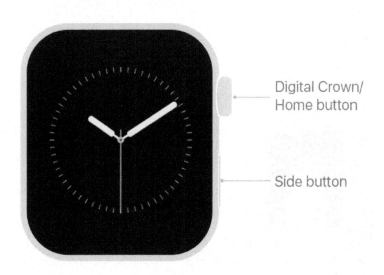

Digital Crown/
Home button

Side button

PRESS THE SIDE BUTTON

- Click to show or hide the Dock.
- Long press to use SOS.
- Double click to use Apple Pay.
- Long press to turn on or off your apple watch.

MAKE USE OF GESTURES

You can use gestures to interact with your Apple Watch. Your watch performs various functions when you touch its screen or press for a long time.

TOUCH

Touch the screen to select a button or an item. On Apple Watch models with Always On, one-touch brings the screen to full brightness.

PRESS AND HOLD

Tap and hold your finger on the watch screen in place to change the watch face, view options in an app, and more.

DRAG

Drag your finger across the screen to scroll or adjust the scroll bar.

SWIPE

Swipe up, down, left, or right to view the different screens.

HOW TO CHANGE THE APPLE WATCH BAND

Follow these steps to remove the strap.

Ensure to make use of a band that matches the size of your Apple Watch case. Case bands 42 mm and 44 mm are compatible with each other, and case ranges 38 mm and 40 mm are compatible with each other.

CHANGE YOUR BAND

- Place the face of your Apple Watch on a clean surface such as a lint-free cloth or a soft cushioned mat.
- If you have a link bracelet, press the quick-release button on one link to separate the band into two pieces.
- Press and hold the band release button on the back, then pull the strap out.

- If the strap does not slide out, press the band release button again and make sure to press it down.

- Make sure the text on the bracelet is in front of you, then pull the new strap inward until you feel and hear a click.

Solo loop

If you have one braided loop or single loop

If you have a Solo Loop or Solo Loop braided, just pull the bottom of the strap to extend it on your wrist when you wear it and take it off.

Milanese loop

Using the Milanese Loop

In 2018, the Milanese Loop has been redesigned so that you can open the strap completely by sliding the magnetic closure over the strap connector or tongue. On previous Milanese Loop models, the closure does not slip through the lug.

Link bracelet

How to remove a link bracelet

The link bracelet must be separated into two pieces before removing the strap from Apple Watch. While loosening the belt, do not force it or twist it. Follow the steps below to avoid damaging the strap or buckle.

1) Close the butterfly lock

If it is open, fold the lock one side at a time till you feel and hear a click.

2) Press and hold the quick-release button

The quick-release buttons are located inside the strap. You simply have to press and hold one.

3) Gently pull the links

Press and hold the quick-release button while dragging. The strap must be separated in two before removing the strap from your Apple Watch.

4) Take off the band

Press and hold the strap release button, then pull the strap out.

NOTE

Never force a band into the slot. If you do not feel or hear a click, move the bar to the left, then to the right. If the bracelet is installed correctly, it will not slide freely until you press and hold the bracelet release button.

If the bar is still unlocked, center it and push it into place. Then carefully move the tape up and down. Don't wear your Apple Watch if the strap slips.

WATCH FACE

You can pick a variety of designs, change colors, and add complications to your apple watch face. You can set the time ahead also.

Change the watch face on Apple Watch

❖ From the watch face, swipe left or right from edge to edge.
❖ Stop when you reach the watch face you want to wear.

Note that not all watch faces are accessible in every country or region. Hermes and Nike watch faces are only available on these models.

Customize the watch face on Apple Watch

❖ Press the digital crown to move to the watch face.
❖ Press and hold the screen.

❖ Swipe left or right to select a watch face, then tap Edit.

❖ Swipe left or right to select a job, then turn the Digital Crown to change it. For example, you can change the color of the second hand or the markings on the watch face.

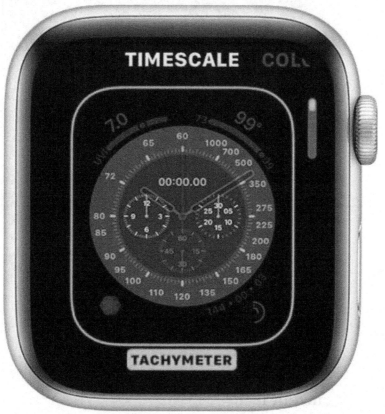

❖ Swipe left to release complications. Touch an additional item to select it, then turn the Digital Crown to change it. You can add complications as well from other applications.

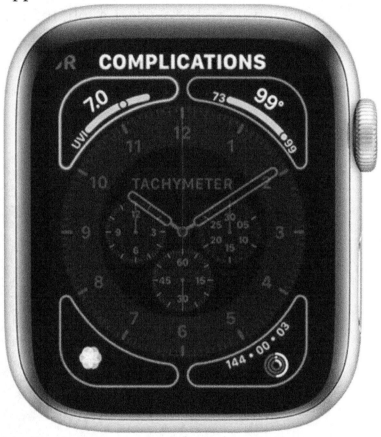

❖ When done, press the Digital Crown to save your changes.
❖ Touch the watch face to set it as your current face.

You can change the watch face as well from your Phone. Head over to the Apple Watch app, simply touches the Face Gallery tab.

Add more information to your watch face

You can add complications or app information to some watch faces. Your Apple Watch has complications that explain battery life, date, and more. You can add complications as well from some third-party applications. To see which apps have complications:

❖ Head over to the Apple Watch application on your iPhone.
❖ Touch the My Watch tab, then touch Complications.

To choose what you want, press Edit, then follow these steps:

1) To add an additional complication, click the "Add" button ⊕. After adding complexity in the Apple Watch app on your iPhone, you can add it to your watch. Return to the Watch screen, touch and hold the screen, then tap Edit. Swipe left to the

49

complications screen. Then touch a complication and turn the Digital Crown to choose what information you want to appear. When done, press the Digital Crown to save your changes. Touch the watch face to set it as your current face.

2) To remove an additional item, click the "Remove" button ⊖. Then press Delete.

Create a new copy of the watch face

❖ Press the digital crown to move to the watch face.

❖ Press and hold the screen, slide your finger all the way to the right, then click the "Add" button on the more icon.
❖ To choose a watch face, turn the Digital Crown, then touch the face you want. This sets the current watch face where you just created it.
❖ To customize the watch face, touch and hold the screen again, then touch Edit.

Remove watch face from Apple Watch

❖ Go to your current watch screen, then tap and hold the screen.
❖ Swipe left or right to the watch face you want to delete.
❖ Swipe up and tap Delete.

If you want, you can recreate the watch face later.

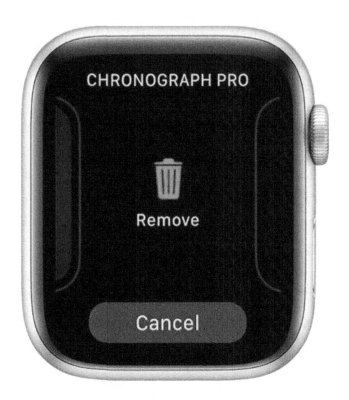

Change the time displayed on Apple Watch

- ❖ Open the Settings app on your watch, then tap the watch.
- ❖ Touch + 0 min.
- ❖ Rotate the Digital Crown and choose the distance you want to set your watch.

❖ Touch Cancel or Set.

You can only preset the time displayed on the watch face. Your alerts, notifications, world clock, and any other time will continue to coincide with real-time.

Hide now playing on Apple Watch

When playing music, Now Playing opens automatically. Here's how to change the settings:

- ❖ Head over to the Settings application on your watch.
- ❖ Touch General> Wake up screen.
- ❖ Disable audio apps that start automatically.

WORKOUT APP

Apple Watch has long been a useful tool for tracking and recording workouts and physical activity.

The new model offers you the ability to add a lot of different workouts and activities for your tracking. And by making use of the Activity application on your Phone, you can see your workout progress and find tips to improve your fitness.

Begin a workout

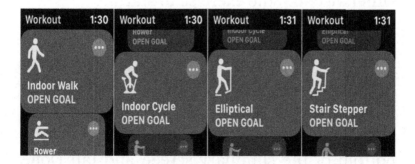

When you are ready to track an exercise or activity, open the Workout app on your watch. Scroll through the different activities until you find the one you want, such as indoor walking, indoor cycling, outdoor jogging, or stairs.

Workout management

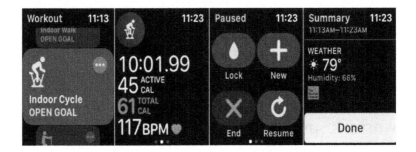

If you want to adjust the workout to a specific number of calories, distance, time, or any other factor, click the ellipsis icon () in the workout and choose the option you want. Otherwise, tap the exercise to start.

Pause the workout at any time by moving the screen to the right and pressing the pause button. When done, swipe left, and click Finish. The summary screen displays total time, calories, and other data. Scroll to the bottom of the summary screen and tap Done to record the workout.

Add workout

Apple Watch offers many virtual exercises; Hiking and yoga were added to the mix in 2018. However, if you don't see the exercise you want, you can choose from a variety of other activities that have been added with watchOS 7.

To do this, scroll to the bottom of the list of exercises and choose the Add Workout option. The screen first lists common workouts and activities, such as basketball, pilates, football, and tennis. Swipe down on the screen to view a variety of other activities and sports in alphabetical order, including archery, bowling, equestrian sports, golf, hockey, jump rope, rowing, tai chi, wrestling, and more.

Workout reminders

You can place reminders on your Watch to tell you to begin and end a workout if the watch detects that you are doing any type of physical activity. This option is automatically enabled, but it can be disabled.

Head over to the Settings application on the apple watch, swipe down and touch workout. Swipe down on the Training screen to display start workout reminders and end workout reminder options; Disable one or both of the reminders by tapping the switch.

The disadvantage is that the workout reminder might take a few mins for it to find out that you are working out and to realize that you have ended a session. Therefore, this

58

job is best for long exercises, such as hiking or cycling.

Record workout

If reminders are enabled and you are in the middle of a workout, your watch would inquire if you would love to record it. Start walking, running, or cycling without telling your watch. If it is attentive, it should find out what activity you are doing and ask if you want to record it.

The request appears as a notification on your watch and offers some options: Workout Record, Workout Change, Silence for the Day, and Decline. You can choose to record the workout if the watch has selected the correct activity. The device will also ask you to stop recording after making sure you have finished the workout.

Workout settings

On the workout screen in the settings, you can enable or disable other options. Power saving mode turns off cellular connectivity and the built-in heart rate sensor during walking/running workouts to extend battery life.

Enable Auto Pause On to automatically pause running workouts when you stop moving and resume when you start moving again. Turn on 'gym equipment discovery' to sync your workouts with compatible gym equipment.

ACTIVITY APP

View activity on Apple Watch

Once you have collected some exercises, you can check your history by applying the activity on your watch. The app displays your current activity in circles and individual charts.

The red movement graph shows the calories you've burned since the start of the day. The green exercise graph indicates the amount of time you have spent exercising so far. The blue holder graph indicates the number of hours you spent on your feet that day. The goal is to close each episode.

Hold down the circle. The next screen allows you to view a weekly summary or change the goal of your movement. By clicking on the weekly summary, you can see a graph of the week, your total calorie count, steps, distance, and other goals you've achieved. Touch the "change" movement goal to increase or decrease the number of calories you want to burn each day.

View activity log

The Activity app on your iPhone provides a lot more data and options than the Watch version. Open the Activity app on your phone. The History tab shows activity info for the present day. Touch the left arrow next to the month at the top of the screen to view the calendar. You can then choose a specific date to display the information for that day.

View activity trends

The new Activity app, introduced by watchOS 6, is the Trends tab. Here, you can check your daily training and activity trends to see how many calories you burn, duration of exercise, duration of standing, and how much distance you travel. The directions also provide advice on how to improve your results for a specific goal. Touch any item to find out more details about it.

View workout history

The "Workouts" tab in the Activity app displays your training activity for that month. Click on a year at the top to see your general workouts for each month, then click on a specific month to scroll down. Click on the All Workouts link at the top and you can filter the list to show only specific exercises.

View awards

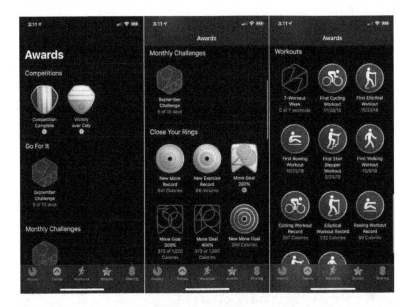

Receive awards based on the achievement of specific practice and activity goals. Click the prizes icon to view your rewards, challenges, and training.

Share activity data

You can challenge a friend to bring their Apple Watch to a fitness competition to encourage both of you. To get started, you must first share your activity data with your friend. Touch the share icon and touch Get started. Press the + button and select the desired person from your contact list.

Touch Send to send the invitation to your friend. The invitation can be accepted by your friend simply by opening the Activity application and clicking **Accept** close to your name. After the person agrees, their name appears on the sharing screen.

Begin a competition

After that, you must invite this person to the challenge. On the Share tab in the Activity app on an iPhone, tap the person's name. Click on the link to compete with this person. Choose the type of competition. And then that person can reply in the Activity app on their iPhone. So let the games begin.

Compare activity data on Apple Watch

Once the competition starts, you can check and compare your activity numbers and the other person. Open the Activity app on your watch. Swipe left to see your stats and yours in the activity partner. Touch the other person's name to find out more details about their numbers.

Compare activity data on iPhone

You can also check the stats on your phone. Open the Activity app on your iPhone. Tap on the share icon. Your screen shows the numbers for you and the other individuals. Click on the person's name to see their stats. Touch their name to see yours.

Complete the competition

When the competition ends, you will receive a notification from your watch. You can also open the Activity app to see the results. The app announces the winner and awards them a badge. Then you can view the final numbers, send a notification to the other individual, invite them to another challenge, or turn the screen off.

PHONE APP

Answer the call

When you hear or feel the call notification, raise your wrist to see who is calling.

Send a call to voicemail: press the red reject button on the incoming call notification.

Answer on your Apple Watch: Press the Answer button to speak using the built-in microphone and speaker, or a Bluetooth device paired with Apple Watch.

Instead, reply with your iPhone or text message: tap the button and then tap an option. If you touch Answer on the Phone, the call would then be placed on hold and the caller would hear a beep continuously till the paired iPhone answers.

If you cannot find the Phone, long touch the bottom of your screen, swipe up, and then touch the Ping Phone button ( ) on the Apple Watch.

70

Apple Watch display when you receive a call the caller's name, the words "incoming call," the red reject button, the green answer button, and more options.

During a call

If you are on a call that does not use Face Time audio, you can switch the call to the iPhone, change the volume of the call, input numbers by making use of the keyboard, and transfer the call to another audio device.

Switch a call from Apple Watch to your iPhone: While talking on your Apple Watch, unlock your iPhone and then press the button or the green bar at the top of the screen.

You can quickly silence an incoming call by pressing the palm of your hand on the watch screen for three seconds. Just make sure Cover to Mute is on: open the Settings app on Apple Watch, tap Sounds & Haptics, then turn on Cover to Mute.

Adjust the call volume: Rotate the digital crown. Click the mute button to mute the end of the call (if you are listening to a conference call, for example).

Enter additional numbers during a call: touch the More button(•••), touch the keypad, then touch Numbers.

Transfer the call to an audio device: tap the More button (•••) and choose a device.

While on a FaceTime Audio call, you can adjust the volume and mute the call by clicking the mute button or by clicking the More button and choosing the audio destination.

72

Turn the Digital Crown to adjust the volume.

Mute the call.

During an incoming phone call, the display shows the horizontal volume indicator in the upper right, the mute button in the lower left, and the red reject button. The duration of the call appears below the name of the caller.

Listen to voicemail

If the caller left a voice message, you will receive a notification; click the "Play" button in the notification to listen. To hear a voicemail later, launch the Phone application on your Apple Watch, afterward touch Voicemail.

On the voicemail screen you have these alternatives:

1. Adjust the volume with the Digital Crown
2. Start and stop playback
3. Jump forward or backward five seconds
4. Call again
5. Delete voicemail

Make phone calls on apple watch

Ask Siri. Say something like:

- Call jerry
- Call 123 456 7891
- Call with mike FaceTime audio

Make a call

- Launch the phone application on the Apple Watch.

- Touch Contacts, then rotate the Digital Crown to scroll.
- Touch the contact you want to call, then touch the phone button.
- Click FaceTime Audio to start a FaceTime audio call or click a phone number.
- Rotate the Digital Crown to adjust the volume during a call.

Note: To reach someone you recently spoke to, click "Recent" and then touch a contact. To call someone you have set as a favorite in the Phone app on your iPhone, tap Favorites and then tap a contact.

Input a phone number on your Apple

- Open the phone application on the Apple Watch.
- Press the keypad, enter the number, then press the call button.

You can also use the keypad to enter additional numbers during a call. Just tap the plus button (***), then tap the keyboard button.

Make calls over Wi-Fi

If your carrier gives Wi-Fi calling, you can make use of your Watch to receive and make calls over Wi-Fi rather than of the cellular network, even when your paired iPhone is off or has been switched off. Your Watch has to be within the Wi-Fi network range that your iPhone has connected to in the past.

To Enable Wi-Fi calling on iPhone:

- On your iPhone, head over to Settings> Phone, touch Wi-Fi Calling, afterward switch on Wi-Fi Calling on this iPhone and add Wi-Fi Calling to other devices.
- Open the phone application on the Apple Watch.
- Choose a contact, then tap the call button.
- Pick the FaceTime address or phone number you want to call.

Note: You can make emergency calls over Wi-Fi, but when possible, use iPhone over a cellular connection; your location information is much more accurate. Ensure your emergency address is recent: On your iPhone, head over to Settings> Phone> Wi-Fi Calling, then touch Update emergency address. If emergency services cannot locate your location, they will go to your emergency address.

View contact information on your Apple Watch

While talking on your iPhone, you can view the contact information on your Apple Watch in the Phone app. You can end the call from your Watch as well (for instance, if you are putting on earphones or headphones).

SLEEP APP

Finally, Apple included a sleep tracking feature on the Apple Watch with the launch of watchOS 7. It's something we've all been calling for since sleep tracking began to be included in all fitness trackers; However, the new Sleep app on the Apple Watch is about a lot more than just sleep tracking. The Sleep application on your Watch aim is to help you create a more regular bedtime practice, and hopefully, it would help you sleep better at night.

It all starts with the new Sleep app included in watchOS 7, and you'll need to set your first sleep schedule to get started.

Set up sleep mode

Before you sleep with the best Apple Watch strap on your wrist, you'll need to run and set up the Sleep app. The first time you launch the Sleep app, you'll be prompted across many different screens to adjust your sleep schedule. You will need to set the time at which you want to wake up and go to bed, set whether you want the alarm, and what sound this alarm will sound, and you will need to select whether you want sleep tracking and enable the disconnect feature. It sounds like a lot, but the process is pretty straightforward - here's how to do it!

- Head over to the Sleep application on your Apple Watch.

- Touch Next. You would have to scroll down to the bottom of your screen.

- Set a target bedtime with the + and - buttons.

- Touch Next. You would have to scroll down to the bottom of your screen.

- Touch every day if you want to choose days for your sleep schedule.

- Touch the days you don't want to be a part of your sleep schedule.

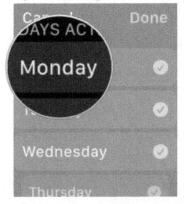

- Touch the time to set the time you want to wake up.

- Touch the alarm on/off switch if you want an alarm.

- Touch the sound to change the sound of the alarm sounds.

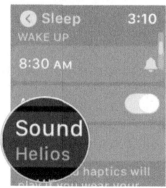

- Touch bedtime to set when you want to go to bed.

- Click Next after reviewing your schedule.

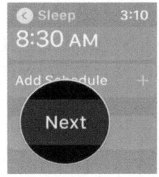

- Tap Enable to allow Apple Watch to track movement while you sleep. You can touch Skip if you don't want this feature.

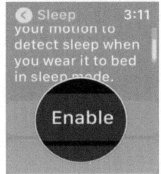

- Adjust the relaxation time with the + and - buttons.

- Touch "Enable" to activate the Wind Down function. You can tap on Skip to switch it off.

- Touch Next.

- Touch Done to finish the setup.

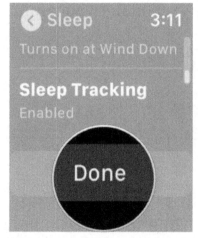

Adjust your sleep schedule

Once you create a sleep schedule, you won't stick to it. You can adjust your sleep schedule at any time by following the steps below.

- Head over to the Sleep application on the Apple Watch.

- Touch the sleep schedule you want to adjust.

- Touch Wake Up Time to set the time you want to wake up.

- Touch the alarm on/off switch if you want an alarm to change the alarm. When the switch is green, the alarm is on.

- Touch sounds and touches to change the sound the alarm makes.

- Play the sound you want.

- Touch Done.

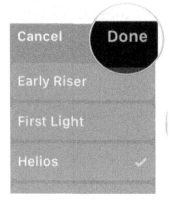

- Touch Bedtime to set the time you want to go to bed.

- Touch Back to return to the main sleep menu.

You can follow these steps to adjust your sleep schedule as many times as you like.

Disable your sleep schedule

Sometimes you might not want to use the sleep schedule or the sleep tracking capabilities of the Apple Watch as you do on vacation, so you'll want to turn off your sleep schedule so that everything shuts down.

- Head over to the Sleep application on the Apple Watch.

- Touch the complete program.

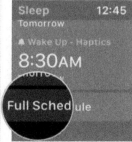

- Touch the sleep schedule on / off switch. When the switch becomes gray, your sleep schedule will be disrupted.

If you have deactivated your sleep schedule for any reason, you can reactivate it with a few clicks by following the same steps described above.

NOISE APP

The Noise app on Apple Watch SE and Apple Watch Series 4 and later measures ambient sound levels in your environment, using a microphone and exposure time. When Apple Watch detects that the decibel level is so high that hearing may be affected, it can notify you by tapping on your wrist.

Keep in mind: The Noise application makes use of the microphone to sample and measure the sound levels in your environs. Apple Watch does not record or save any sound to measure these levels.

Set up the noise application

- Head over to the Noise application on your Watch.
- Touch Enable to activate supervision.
- To measure the ambient noise around you in the future, open the Noise app, or use noise complication.

Get noise alert

- Head over to the Settings application on the Apple Watch.
- Go to Noise> Noise Notifications and then choose a setting.

You can launch the Apple Watch application as well on the iPhone, touch My Watch, and afterward head over to Noise> Noise Threshold.

View information about ambient sound levels

- Head over to the Health application on your Phone.
- Click Browse, click Hearing, and then click the environmental sound level.

Turn off noise measurement

- Head over to the Settings application on your Watch.
- Go to Noise> Ambient Sound Measurements.
- Turn off measure sounds.

You can launch the Apple Watch application as well on your iPhone, then touch My Watch, afterward touch Noise, and then turn the environmental sound measurement off.

93

MEMOJI APP

The full list of WatchOS 7 features includes a completely new Memoji app. Thanks to this, you can now create custom Memoji directly from your Apple Watch. Create multiple avatars for different moods, send them in messages, or turn them into the watch face.

Create a Memoji

- On Apple Watch, open the Memoji app.

- Press "+" to create a new Memoji. Press the memoji app and then press the plus sign on the Apple Watch.

- Here you would see different options such as eyes, hair, skin, etc. Click on each feature and use the Digital Crown to scroll and choose your preferred option.

- The chosen option will be displayed on your new Memoji. You can also click on Meomji to see his various expressions.

- Once you're satisfied, tap Done to add Memoji to your collection.

And that is! Your Memoji is ready to go. But that's not all, you can modify and use Memoji on your Apple Watch, at any time and in any way you want.

Edit Memoji is present

- Open the Memoji app
- Touch the Memoji you plan on editing
- Select the function and use the Digital Crown to scroll and choose a theme.
- Click Done to save your changes.

Duplicate Memoji

You want to have several Memoji on hand, just repeat them and make the necessary changes.

- Open the Memoji app

- Tap on Memoji

- Scroll down to the bottom
- Select Duplicate Memoji.

Now, open up your refined Memoji and edit it.

Delete Memoji

- Open Memoji app
- Tap on Memoji

- Scroll down to the bottom

- Choose Delete Memoji to get rid of it.

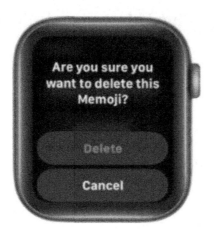

Create a Memoji watch face

- In the Memoji app

- Select Memoji and scroll down to **create a watch face**.

- Click on the option and exit the application.

Memoji will automatically become the current watch face. If it does not, press and hold the current watch face and then swipe left to find and select a Memoji watch face.

In particular, this watch face will also be added to the suite of Apple Watch applications on the iPhone. So you can easily share it from watch or iPhone.

Use Memoji in Messages on Apple Watch

- Head over to the Messages application and choose the conversation.
- Press the Memoji button, and choose the image from the Memoji sticker set to see how it looks.
- Just tap on Memoji and it will be sent.

HANDWASHING FEATURE

With watchOS 7, Apple introduced a new feature called Hand Wash Detection. After enabling it, when you wash your hands and put on your Apple Watch, it will start a 20-second automatic timer. If you stop washing your hands before the end of 20 seconds, you will be prompted to continue. Apple calls it "the first innovation of its kind in a portable device." Besides that, it can also remind you to wash your hands when you get home.

Apple Watch that supports hand washing

- Apple Watch Series 4
- Apple Watch Series 5
- Apple Watch Series 6 and SE

Important Note: Although Apple Watch Series 3 is compatible with watchOS 7, it does not have hand washing.

How to enable watchOS 7 handwash detection

- Touch the Digital Crown and touch the Settings app icon

- Scroll down with Touch or Digital Crown. Tap Hand wash

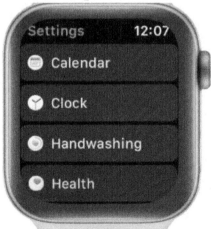

- Turn on the timer toggle button to activate the hand wash feature on Apple Watch.

- Haptics is enabled by default. But, you can decide to deactivate it

Now, Apple Watch will use motion sensors, a microphone (to detect the sounds of running water), and machine learning on the device to automatically know when to start washing hands.

Test Handwashing detection on Apple Watch

Start washing your hands and this function will work automatically. A 20-second counter will appear on the screen.

If you stop before twenty seconds, your Apple Watch will ask you to continue. Once this is done, you will feel haptic reactions (if left enabled) and hear a sound.

How to check hand washing data in the Health app on iPhone

The Health app on iPhone syncs your hand washing data and displays it too. Here's how to view it and add it to your favorites.

- Head over to the Health application on your iOS 14 device

- Click Browse
- Click Other Data

- Click Handwashing to view handwashing data in the Health app on an iPhone running iOS 14
- If you want to see this information in the summary on the main screen of the Health app, scroll down and tap Add to favorites.

HEART RATE APP

Heart rate is an important way to monitor how your body works. You can monitor your heart rate during a workout; view your rest, walking, breathing, training, and recovery rates throughout the day; or do a new reading at any time.

View your heart rate

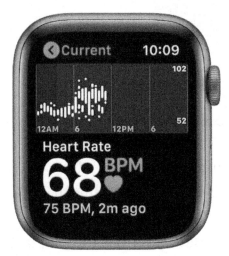

- Head over to the Heart Rate application on your Watch to view your present heart rate, resting rate, and average walking rate.

Your Apple Watch continues to measure your heart rate while you wear it.

Monitor your heart rate during a workout

By default, your current heart rate is shown in the multi-metric workout view. To customize the metrics that will be displayed during a workout, follow these steps:

- Head over to the Apple Watch application on your Phone.
- Touch My Watch, go to Training> Training View, then touch a workout.

Monitor your heart rate with a glance.

View a graph of heart rate data

- Head over to the Health application on your iPhone.
- Touch Explore at the bottom right, touch Heart, then touch Heart rate.
- To add your heart rate to the summary, swipe up and then tap Add to favorites.

You can see your heart rate in the last hour, day, week, month, or year. Tap on Show more heart rate data and you can also view your heart rate range for the chosen time period; your rest, walking, training, and breathing rate; and any notification of high or low heart rate.

Activate heart rate data
By default, Apple Watch monitors the Heart Rate app's heart rate, workouts, and breathing sessions. If you turned off heart rate data, you can turn it back on.

- Head over to the Settings application on your Watch.
- Go to Privacy> Health.

- Touch Heart rate, then turn on Heart rate.

You can also open the Apple Watch app on your iPhone, tap My Watch, Privacy, and then turn on your heart rate.

Receive notifications about high or low heart rate

Your Apple Watch can warn you if your heart rate stays above a certain threshold or below a certain threshold after it has been inactive for at least 10 minutes. You can switch the heart rate notifications on when you open the heart rate application for the first time or at any time after.

- Head over to the Settings application on your Watch, then touch Heart.
- Touch High heart rate notifications or Low heart rate notifications, then set a heart rate threshold.

You can launch the Apple Watch application on your iPhone as well, simply touch My Watch, and then Heart. Touch High heart rate or Low heart rate, and then set a threshold.

Receive notifications about irregular heart rhythms

You may be notified if Apple Watch has identified an irregular heart rhythm that appears to be atrial fibrillation (AFib).

- Head over to the Settings application on your Watch

- Tap Heart and turn on irregular rhythm notifications.

You can launch the Apple Watch application as well on your iPhone, touch My Watch, touch Heart, and then turn Irregular Rhythm on.

Keep in mind: For the best outcome, make sure the back of the Apple Watch is in contact with your skin for features like touch notifications, blood oxygen measurements, pulse detection, (Apple Watch Series 6 only), and heart rate sensor. Putting on your Watch with the perfect fit - not too baggy, or too tight and with room for the skin to breathe - make it comfortable and lets the sensors to do their work.

CYCLE TRACKING

In Apple Watch, apple added cycle tracking, a women's health tracking feature that lets you record your monthly periods, pre- and post-menstrual symptoms, and whatever else you want to monitor to plan your future family or plan not to start one. The Health app is where you can set up and start tracking your monthly cycle data, but you can also track your daily symptoms and monthly activity on your Apple Watch. Data from the health app is synced to your Apple Watch, so you can receive notifications about your next expected period or fertility days, record symptoms or periods, and more.

Set up your monthly cycle data in the Health application on iPhone

To start tracking your monthly cycle, you just need to add a few details to the Health app.

- Head over to the Health application on iPhone.

- Touch the search tab.

- Select Cycle Tracking.

- Touch Options just above the cycle log.

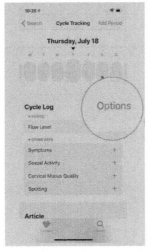

- Scroll down and tap Period duration and enter the period duration.

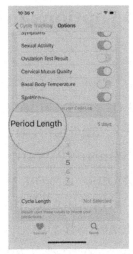

- Touch Cycle length and enter the average amount of time you have between periods.

This info lets the Health application create a prediction and fertility calendar based on when your period begins.

Customize cycle tracking options in Health app on iPhone

You can select which aspects of your cycle you want to record each day, week, and month. If you are trying to conceive, you may want to include all the cycle log options. If you just want to keep track of when you should have your period again, you can leave all the cycle recording options. This is where to find them.

- Head over to the Health application on iPhone.

- Touch the Browse tab.

- Select Cycle Tracking.

- Touch Options just above the cycle log.

119

- Enable or disable symptoms to display the selected symptoms in the Health app log. Symptoms include.

  Abdominal cramps

  Acne

  Changes in appetite

  Swelling

  Tender breasts

  Constipation

  Diarrhea

  Headache

  Hot flushes

  Lumbar back pain

  Humor changes

  Nausea

  Pain in ovulation

  Fatigue

  Sleep changes

- Activate the Sexual activity switch to display your recorded sexual activity.
- Enable the Ovulation test results option to display the recorded ovulation test results.
- Activate the Cervical Mucus Quality switch to display the recorded cervical mucus data.
- Turn on the basal body temperature switch to display the recorded temperature.
- Enable spotting to display recorded spotting incidents.

Register a period for cycle tracking in the Health app on iPhone

Now that you are ready and ready to go, it's time to start tracking your cycle. The next time your period starts, add it to the Health app. You can also add data from the previous month's period if you want to start your cycle forecast calendar right away.

- Head over to the Health application on iPhone.
- Touch the Browse tab.
- Select Cycle Tracking.

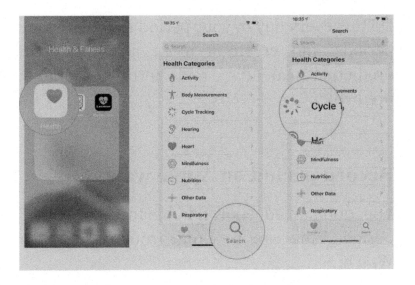

- Touch the day in the daily tracker on top of the data summary.
- Or tap Add period in the upper right corner of the screen, then select a date.
- Touch Period in the Menstruation section to record the menstrual flow for the day.
- Touch Done.

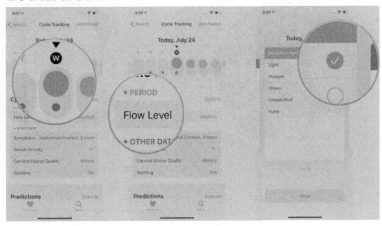

Do this every day of your period to record your periods and create a more accurate cycle prediction calendar and fertility window predictor.

Record period on Apple watch

You don't need your iPhone to record your period. This can be done from your Apple Watch.

- Press the digital crown on your Apple Watch to charge the taskbar.
- Touch the Cycle Tracking application.
- Touch the day in the daily tracker on top of the data summary.

- Touch Period in the Menstruation section to record the menstrual flow for the day.
- Touch Done.

Record a cycle symptom in Apple Watch

Just like recording your period, you can also record your period symptoms every day, right on your Apple Watch.

- Press the digital crown on your Apple Watch to charge the taskbar.
- Touch the Cycle Tracking application.
- Touch Symptoms.
- Pick all symptoms that are applicable to you from the list.
- Touch Done.

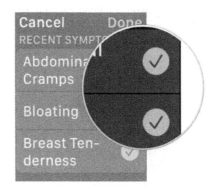

From your Apple Watch, you can also add data on cervical mucus viscosity, sexual activity for the day, and whether or not you experienced spotting.

Delete Cycle Tracking Data in Health App on iPhone

Actually, it is surprisingly difficult to figure out how to delete the data. If you made a mistake in one of your registration activities and want to completely delete your data, you will need to take a few steps to get there.

- Head over to the Health application on the iPhone.

126

- Touch the Browse tab.
- Select Cycle Tracking.

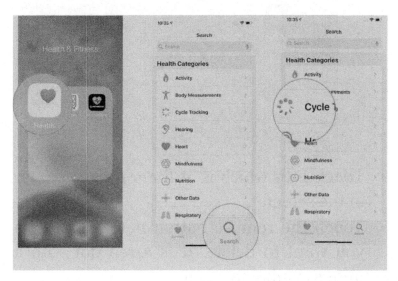

- Scroll down and select View Cycle Tracking Items.
- Select the category record you want to delete.
- Scroll down and pick Show all data.

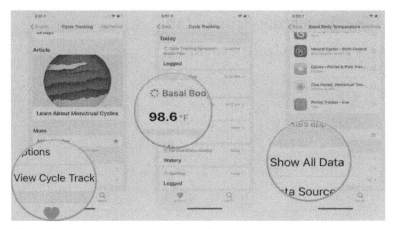

- Touch Edit which is at the top right corner of the screen.
- Touch the remove button next to the data you want to delete. It is a red dot with a minus symbol inside it.
- Touch Delete.
- Touch Done.

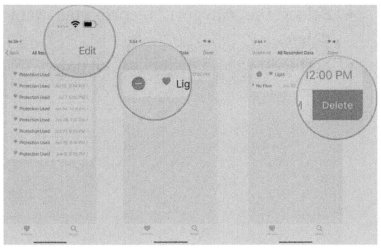

Do this for any logged data that you want to remove from the cycle trace.

Delete the cycle tracker app

Not everybody needs the Cycle Tracking application. So, you can simply delete the app and erase its existence from your wrist just like you would any third-party app.

Head over to the home screen of the Apple Watch and:

- If the app layout is set to List view, swipe left on the Cycle Tracking app and then tap the red bin.
- If the app layout is set to grid view, press and hold the Cycle Monitor app until it enters jiggly mode, then tap the X to remove it.

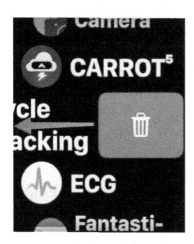

SIRI

Just like when you set up Siri on the iPhone, making Siri appear on your Apple Watch is a breeze. It's normal to make sure your device is online so that Siri can get the information, although the voice assistant is already inside the clock and ready to go just by setting things up from the connected iPhone.

Set up Siri on Apple Watch

To modify Siri settings on Apple Watch, follow these steps:

- On Apple Watch, go to Settings> General> Siri to toggle "Hello Siri" and "Volume up to talk" on and off.
- If you have a Watch Series 3 or Series 4, simply scroll down to Voice Annotations in the Settings section to control whether Siri speaks to you. The Assistant can be set to respond all the time and only respond when you have headphones in sleep mode.

131

- If you have Siri voice response enabled, the volume will match the volume within the Alerts tab in the Sounds and Haptics section of the Apple Watch; adjust it if desired.
- If you want to change Siri's voice, do so with your iPhone, as the pair must have identical volume charts. Go to Siri & Search> Siri Voice and select one; The next time your Apple Watch syncs with your phone, it should update automatically.

Activate Siri on Apple Watch

So here's how to set up and edit when Siri responds to you, but how do you ask Siri a question on an Apple Watch? Well, again, everything is very simple and there are actually several ways to do it.

Press the digital crown

The easiest way to wake up Siri is to press and hold the Digital Crown; Once you do it for a few seconds, the listening indicator will

132

appear and you can release it. This is the best way to wake Siri without making a sound, although you will obviously have to speak for it to respond, as Apple does not offer the ability to write or edit requests on the watch.

Say "Hey Siri"

An easy way to activate Siri hands-free is to simply say hello to the voice assistant. All you have to do here is make sure the screen is on before greeting Siri, and you should see her wake up and show the Listen indicator.

Raise your wrist

Simply raise your wrist and alert your Apple Watch before holding it close to your mouth; the Listen indicator should appear automatically if the feature is enabled in Settings> General> Siri> Lift to speak on the watch.

Apple Watch Siri Commands

- Hey Siri, what time is it at [location]?

- Hey Siri, start a 30 minute run for me
- Hey Siri, turn down the volume by 40%
- Hey Siri, what is the weather at [location]?
- Hey Siri, how is my day?
- Hey Siri, turn on Airplane mode.
- Hey Siri, set a timer for [time] from minutes.
- Hey Siri, send a message to my dad.
- Hey Siri, call [Contact].
- Hey Siri, get directions to [place or location].
- Hey Siri, turn my lights on."

Add Siri to the face of your Apple Watch

There is actually a fourth way to access Siri from the Apple Watch, choosing Siri as the complication. These complications, to begin with, are the little customizable tools on the Apple Watch's home screen.

With Siri as one of your complications, as shown above, all you have to do is tap on the icon and wait for the Listen cursor to appear.

Well, there is also a Siri clock face for you to explore, which is packed with information cards (including local weather, sunset/sunrise time, and your reminders) that Siri thinks might be helpful for you to jump right into or see in an instant. And with the introduction of Siri Shortcuts in the latest versions of iOS and watchOS, the suggestions Siri offers have been vastly improved.

BREATHE

Apple's new Breathe app aims to improve our mental state, which is what hours of standing/rolling have done for our bodies.

When you feel stressed, your breathing goes up to your chest and becomes shallow and rapid. Historically, this was useful when you were extremely anxious, about to fight or run for your life. Today, most of our high anxiety situations do not benefit from an adrenaline rush and fight or flight responses.

Enter Breathe, an Apple app that is built into watchOS. The application helps to return to a calm state with regular deep breathing from the stomach. It signals the brain to relax, restore a calm state, and become calmer.

Why breath?

Deep breathing is one of the easiest tools you can use to reduce stress levels in your body. When you breathe deeply and slowly, you send a message to your brain that everything is fine and that the brain does not need to release adrenaline (adrenaline) to fight or escape. Rather, taking deep breaths activates the hypothalamus, which sends a notification to the pituitary gland to hold back stress hormones and trigger a relaxation response in the parasympathetic nervous system. In other words, long, deep breathing tells your brain that all is well, that you are not in danger, that you do not have to release stress hormones, and that you can relax.

Making use of the Breathe app

The application serves as a guide for you through a series of deep breathing techniques to help you better manage daily stress. It does this through animations on the watch face, as well as haptic feedback on your wrist. It urges you to inhale and exhale with notes of how long each inhales and exhale should last.

- Head over to the Breathe application on your Watch.

- Use the Digital Crown to set the number of minutes you want to breathe (and the breaths you want to take).
- Press the start button.
- Follow the animation on the clock face.

At the end of the session, you will get a reading of your breathing time and your current heart rate after the breathing exercises.

COMPASS

The Compass app known as the Compass icon displays the direction the Apple Watch is facing; Your present location, And elevation.

Keep in mind: If you delete the Compass application from your iPhone, it would also be erased from Apple Watch.

View your coordinates, incline, elevation, and bearing

Your address is displayed in the upper left. Rotate the digital crown to scroll up to view the tilt, elevation, and coordinates.

- Open the Compass app and the Compass icon on your Apple Watch.
- For accurate directions, hold the Apple Watch flat to align the sight on the center of the compass.
- To add direction, rotate the Digital Crown to scroll up, tap Add bearing, turn Apple Watch towards bearing, and then tap Done.

- To release bearing, rotate the digital crown to scroll up, tap Edit heading, switch Apple Watch to the new heading, and then tap Done.
- To clear the bearing, turn the Digital Crown to scroll up, then touch Clear Bearing.

Crosshairs aligned

Add elevation complication to the watch face Apple Watch Series 6

The always-on altimeter on Apple Watch Series 6 lets you track your current altitude in real-time. Add elevation complication to the watch face to see the height at a glance.

- With the watch face displayed, touch and hold the screen, then touch Edit.
- Swipe left all the way.
  If there is a complication face, it will be displayed on the last screen.
- Touch a complication to select it, rotate the digital crown to the compass, then choose Elevation.
- Press the digital crown to save your changes, then touch the face to switch to it.

Note: The compass will not display altitude or coordinates if location services are disabled. To turn off or on-location services, head over to the Settings application on your Watch, touch Privacy, afterward touch Location Services.

To use True North rather than Magnetic North, head over to the Settings application on your Watch, touch the Compass, and then turn **Use True North** on.

Note: On some watch straps, the compass can be affected by magnetic materials.

MEASURE BLOOD OXYGEN LEVEL WITH APPLE WATCH

The Apple Watch Series 6 has a new built-in sensor that can measure the oxygen level in the blood. This is perhaps the biggest innovation and could have real benefits in judging the health and reacting to the first signs of conditions like heart failure, asthma, and coronavirus.

How the Apple Watch measures oxygen levels

To make oxygen measurements possible, Apple changed the design of the sensors on the bottom of the Apple Watch with the Series 6. Apple has also added additional red LEDs and some additional photodiodes.

The principle of oxygenometry is the same or similar to that of pulse oximetry: the four groups of LEDs illuminate the skin and basic vessels, the photodiodes record the reflected background light, and can use algorithms to calculate the amount of oxygen that red blood cells are currently being transported within the body. This calculation is based on knowing that the more oxygen is attached to the red blood cells, the redder the blood will appear. The protein responsible for binding to oxygen, hemoglobin, contains iron-containing compounds that can bind to oxygen molecules. When paired, the color changes from dark red to bright red and this change can be captured through the Apple Watch's photodiodes.

An additional app is required on the Apple Watch to take measurements. This application guides the user through the measurement and displays the measured data. This information is also added to the Health app in the new Blood Oxygen tab.

What the information can tell you

According to Apple, normal blood oxygen saturation should be 95 to 99 percent, but this limit is slightly lower for some people. Even during sleep, saturation can drop below the 95 percent threshold.

The ability to know how much oxygen is in the blood has important medical tools because it can help identify heart failure when the heart cannot adequately pump blood through the body, as is the case with perinatal cardiomyopathy (PPCM). It can also warn of an asthma attack and can indicate if you have respiratory problems associated with the coronavirus.

What do you need

Apple Watch Series 6 is the only Apple Watch capable of measuring oxygen in the blood.

It has to be running watchOS 7 and the paired iPhone would have to be running iOS 14.

Apple indicated that oxygen measurement will only be available in some countries, but has not yet confirmed which countries will have the app that has the ability to measure oxygen

144

in the blood. When Apple released the Apple Watch Series 4 with the ability to take an ECG, the feature was initially not available in the UK. The UK had to wait until 2019 to get the feature as Apple needed to scan the app for use in the European Economic Area. Hopefully, this is not the case with blood oxygen monitoring.

Similar to the ECG app, the Oxygen app is only activated for users over 18 years of age. Users must also be 18 or older to share Apple Watch data with a family member's iPhone.

Measure blood oxygen with Apple Watch

Before you can take the first measurement, you must prepare the application.

- Open the Health app on iPhone.
- Click on the Discovery tab.
- Select airways.
- Choose oxygen saturation and activate it.

To make sure the app works reliably, Apple recommends taking the measurement while sitting

Your hand should not move, the watch should sit firmly on the wrist and not slip.

The measurement takes fifteen seconds, after which it will show a percentage of the oxygen content in the blood.

How to take background measurements

The watch can measure the blood oxygen content in the background even without opening the app.

This happens usually when the individual using it is not moving.

For Apple Watch to take measurements while sleeping, the user must activate the sleep plan in the Health app.

The results of all background measurements can be viewed in the Health application in the Respiratory area. Since red light can be a nuisance in the dark, the watch app allows the user to disable background metering. You can do this in theater mode.

ECG

The ECG notification and irregular rhythm features were first announced in September 2018, along with the ECG feature of the Apple Watch Series 4, although it is also available on Watch Series 5 and Watch Series 6.

The arrhythmia notification feature checks the heart rhythms in the background every two hours and sends a notification if an irregular heartbeat is detected.

For those unfamiliar with the term, an electrocardiogram, short for electrocardiogram, is a method of measuring the timing and strength of the electrical signals that make up the heartbeat. By reading the ECG, the doctor can see your heart rate and any irregularities, and intervene if needed

Supported country

The ECG app is available in the United States, Chile, Puerto Rico, Guam, the US Virgin Islands, the United Kingdom, New Zealand, and 19 countries in Europe.

Set up the Apple Watch ECG app

- iOS 12.2 and WatchOS 5.2
- Open the Health app

Make sure you are running iOS 12.2 or later and WatchOS 5.2 or later, after which you will be able to access the ECG function in the Health app on your phone.

If you are doing this for the first time, you should see a message asking you to configure it. If not, go to Health data> Heart> Electrocardiogram (ECG). Setup is very easy and requires some details, such as age. That's because an ECG is not recommended before the age of 22.

Once set up, you can open the Apple Watch ECG app and start taking ECG.

Take an ECG on Apple Watch

- Open the ECG app on Apple Watch Series 6

149

- Place your index finger on the Digital Crown
- Wait 30 seconds

Once the app is set up, you can take the ECG anytime and anywhere you want.

Simply open the ECG app on the watch, place your arm on something to reduce movement, and place your index finger (from the arm without the watch) on the digital crown. It is not necessary to press the digital crown. It's about making redundant communication so that the system controls what happens.

The test around 30 secs to complete, then you would see a representation of your heart rate on your screen. When finished, Apple Watch will give you an instant result, along with the ability to record any symptoms you were feeling at the time.

Meanwhile, on your iPhone, you will receive a notification with a link to the report directly so that you can view more details or share the results with your doctor.

Meaning of Apple Watch ECG results

Once you have finished capturing your EGC reading, you will receive one of four messages.

- For Sinus rhythm, it means that everything is as expected.
- Atrial fibrillation means that an irregular pattern has been detected.
- A low or high heart rate is the third possible result
- An inconclusive result means the test cannot determine the final result.

Sharing your ECG result

To do this, go to the Health app> Browse> Touch Heart> Electrocardiogram (ECG)> ECG Result.

You can then export the details via PDF to share with your doctor.

Apple does not share this information with anyone else, such as a third-party insurance company, other apps, or even your computer.

FALL DETECTION

The fall detection feature built into Apple Watch is a powerful resource in times of stress. When this happens, the wearable device automatically touches your wrist, sounds an alarm, and displays an alert. From there you can decide whether to call emergency services (from the watch, of course) or dismiss the warnings.

With fall detection, Apple Watch is intuitive enough to know whether or not you're moving. After falling, it will wait for it to stop to respond to the alert. If you are stationary and not moving, the watch will automatically call emergency services if you do not respond within 60 seconds.

Then you will see a 30-second countdown on your watch until the time of the automatic call. You can click "Cancel" at any time to stop the countdown.

After you call emergency services, individuals on your emergency contact list would get a notification showing that a fall has happened.

153

It would also show them your present location.

What happens during an emergency call?

During your call to emergency personnel, your Apple Watch will play a voice message informing them that your Apple Watch has detected a fall. From there, you will also share your longitude and latitude coordinates. This looping message will continue to play until you touch Stop Recorded Message. When this happens, you can have a conversation with the respondent. As mentioned above, once you are done with your call, tap on the phone icon to end the call. Click "Yes" to confirm.

How to activate fall detection

Fall detection on Apple Watch Series is disabled by default unless you are 65 or older.

From Apple Support Document: If you input your age when setting up your Apple

Watch or in the Health application and your age is 65 or older, this feature is automatically turned on.

To make sure your Apple Watch is ready for fall detection, you can manually activate fall detection from your iPhone.

- Head over to the Watch application on your iPhone.
- Click on the My Watch tab at the bottom left.
- Click on Emergency SOS.
- Scroll down and turn on fall detection. Shift to the right when running.

Making an emergency call after a fall

When you fall and receive an alert on your Apple Watch, you will see a slider to call emergency services next to the I'm okay button.

- To call emergency services, move the slider from left to right on Apple Watch. If you're not hurt, tap I'm fine.
- Follow the instructions of the emergency service operator.
- Click on the phone icon once you are done with your call to end the call.
- Click "Yes" to confirm.

Remember, you can also make an emergency call anytime on Apple Watch and iPhone using Emergency SOS.

Adding friends and family to your emergency contact list

You can create emergency contacts with the Health app on iPhone. To add emergency contacts, follow these instructions:

- Head over to the Health application on your iPhone.
- Your profile should be at the top right corner simply tap on it.
- Click Medical ID.
- Touch Edit which is at the top right corner.
- Scroll down to the Emergency Contacts section and click Add Emergency Contact, which will open your iPhone's contact list.
- Touch the contact you want to add to your emergency contact list.
- From there, you will need to click on the phone number of the contact you want to use.
- Next, define your relationship with this person.

From here, you will return to the Edit Medical ID screen. Click Add Emergency Contact to add another person to your list. Repeat steps 4-6 above.

Settings to be enabled for fall detection to work

You must have wrist detection enabled for Apple Watch to call emergency services automatically.

- Head over to the Settings application on the Apple Watch.
- Tap on Passcode.
- Scroll to the bottom and turn wrist detection on.

How to disable fall detection

The fall detection feature of Apple Watch Series 4 is disabled by default unless you are 65 years of age or older.

If for some reason, you decide that you do not want the fall detection feature to be activated, you can deactivate it in the Watch app on your iPhone.

- Head over to the Watch application on your iPhone.
- Click on the My Watch tab at the bottom left.
- Click on Emergency SOS.
- Scroll down and disable fall detection. Shift left when closed.

APPLE PAY

Apple Watch is one of the easiest ways to use your Apple Watch on the go. To add new credit or debit cards to your apple watch for purchase, adhere to these guidelines.

Set up and add cards to Apple Pay

To use Apple Pay and make a payment on your Apple Watch, your bank must support the payment service. You can find the most recent information about participating Apple Pay banks on the Apple Support website. You can adhere to the guidelines as well to add new cards and confirm whether your bank supports the protocol.

- Had over to the Watch application on your iPhone.
- Touch the My Watch tab.
- Touch Wallet & Apple Pay.
- Click Add card under Payment cards.

- Touch "Continue."
- Click enter card details manually or place the iPhone over your credit card to scan the information.
- Add the security code of your card.
- Touch Next.
- Touch Add.
- Touch "Confirm" to confirm the terms and conditions of your bank.
- Touch a text message, email, or contact to send yourself a verification message.
- Touch Next.
- Enter the verification code you received.

161

- Touch Next.
- Touch "Done" when finished.

Your bank card is would now be accessible with Apple Pay on your Watch. Depending on your bank, you may receive a confirmation via text message, email, or letter in the mail.

Note: Adding an Apple Pay card to Apple Watch does not add it to use on your iPhone. You will need to add it to your phone separately.

Making use of Apple Pay on Apple Watch

To make an Apple Pay payment with your Apple Watch using your default card:

1. To use your default card, double-click the side button, and hold the Apple Watch screen a few inches from the contactless reader.

2. Wait until you feel a soft touch to confirm the push. To return to the watch face simply Press the Digital Crown.

Making use of a different card to make a purchase:

- Double-tap the side button on the watch.
- Swipe left or right to choose the card you want to use. Once you have this card on the watch face, place your watch near the reader for payment.
- Wait until you feel a soft touch to confirm the push. To return to the watch face simply Press the Digital Crown.

TIPS AND TRICKS

There are so many cool things you can do with your Apple Watch besides checking the time or texting: Here are some awesome tips and tricks about this new wearable on your wrist!

Wake up to the last application used

By default, when you move your wrist, your Apple Watch will wake up and show the time. If you'd rather go back to what you were doing before bed, you can change this setting by going to Settings> General> Wake Up Screen.

From here scroll down to the On-Screen Raise Show the Last section. Options include during sessions, within two minutes of last use, within one hour of last use, and always.

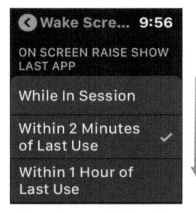 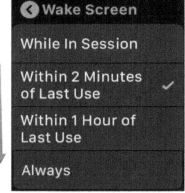

Enlarge the text on the screen

With such a small device, sometimes you want to have a larger text option at your disposal. This can be easily done in the Accessibility settings; To change the text on the apple watch, head over to Settings> Brightness and Text Size, and adjust the way you like.

You can also choose a large text clock display if all you care about is viewing the time in large quantities.

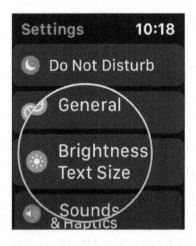 

Silence alerts with the palm of your hand

If your watch has sound enabled, you can prevent it from disturbing the outside world with notification sounds - if it rings somewhere you don't prefer, you can cover the screen with your hand for three seconds or more to instantly silence any new sounds. To operate this, you will need to visit the Apple Watch app on your iPhone and then go to My Watch> Sounds and Haptics> Cover to mute.

Hide clock apps

To prevent third-party apps from appearing on the Apple Watch, go to the Apple Watch app on your iPhone and make sure you're in the My Watch section. Scroll to the bottom to the section known as Installed on your Watch. Touch the apps you want to remove by turning them off. Even if you have removed your watch faces, these apps will still be installed on your iPhone unless you remove them from that device as well.

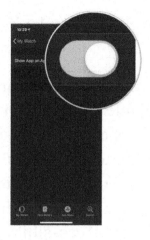

Find an iPhone using your watch

Can't find your iPhone? Don't worry, Apple Watch can help you track it. From the watch face, swipe up to activate Control Center. From here, press the blue Ping button on the iPhone to make it make noise.

Quick access to Zoom and VoiceOver

Do you want Zoom or VoiceOver to be quickly available on your watch? You can enable the triple-click accessibility shortcut to automatically activate Zoom or VoiceOver mode. To do this, visit the Apple Watch app on your iPhone, then go to My Watch> General> Accessibility> Accessibility shortcut. From here, you can choose what you want to automatically activate with a triple-click.

Siri can turn on or off VoiceOver as well with a simple command; simply ask your watch.

Take a screenshot

Do you want to remember a digital tactile drawing or the completion of the activity? You can take a screenshot on Apple Watch by quickly and simultaneously pressing the side button and the digital crown.

Force restart Apple Watch

If your watch is malfunctioning, you can turn it off by pressing and holding the side button until you see the Power off slider, then drag it across the screen. If your watch is completely frozen, you can perform a force restart by pressing the side button and the digital crown for at least ten seconds, until you see the Apple logo.

Set your watch in just five minutes

Do you like to be early for your appointments? You can manually set the watch face to display at a speed of five minutes; This will not affect alerts, notifications, or clocks for other countries, but will show up on the watch face. For this to be done, head over to Settings> Time> +0 minutes, afterward rotate the Digital Crown to advance the time to 59 minutes.

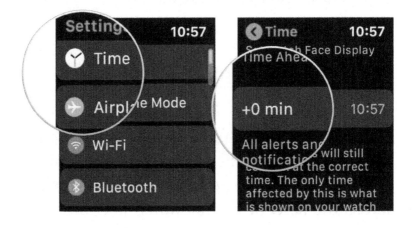

Turn off the snooze of your alarms

You can disable the snooze button on the Apple Watch by going to the Alarm app on the device and tapping the alarm time you want to change. Then toggle the snooze option.

Create custom message responses in advance

You can't type directly on Apple Watch, but you can set up some pre-configured responses through your iPhone that you can tap during conversations to automatically send. To do so, visit the Apple Watch app and go to My Watch> Messages> Default Replies. You can change this list and add/remove preconfigured responses at any time.

Always send your text as voice

When you reply to a message with your voice, Apple Watch offers one of two options: send it as dictated text or send your dictation as an audio clip. If you prefer to always send your messages as audio clips or always as a signal, you can achieve this by visiting the Apple Watch app on your iPhone, then go to My Watch> Messages> Audio Messages.

Place a call on hold until you find your iPhone

While making phone calls on the Apple Watch is a very futuristic feeling, it isn't always practical. If you get a call on your watch and you want to answer it, but your phone is not at hand and you don't want to start it on your watch, you can tap Answer on iPhone to hold the call until you find your device. The person on the other end will hear a short beep repeatedly until you can access their iPhone.

Turn on Walkie-Talkie

You must activate the Walkie-Talkie feature on your Apple Watch to use it. To do this, go to the Walkie-Talk application on the handheld device and turn on the switch provided. Otherwise, people will not be able to communicate with you using the tool.

Clear all notifications with Force Touch

Although you can swipe left to remove an individual notification from the notification screen, you can also get rid of all notification alerts with one click. First, swipe down from the screen to access notifications, then firmly tap the screen to bring up the Clear all option.

Mark emails with Force Touch

There is no way to create a new email on the watch due to its relative uselessness as an email device, but you can easily flag messages that you want to reply to later. Just press firmly on an email message, then tap **Flag**.

Choose which mailboxes will appear on your watch

Don't want to be inundated with notifications and information from all of your mailboxes? You can choose specific mailboxes to appear on the clock from the iPhone app. Simply head over to My Watch> Mail> Include Mail.

Switch between day and List views on the calendar

Want to see what your day looks like, but also display items in a list? You can switch between day and Calendar List views using the onscreen Force Touch gesture while in the app.

Build your leaving time in the calendar alerts

If a location has been added to your event, you can create an alert to notify you when these

175

factors are left in the driving or walking distance along with traffic. To do this, make sure the "Travel time" switch is enabled in the individual event; You can do this on your iPhone by going to the Calendar app, clicking on the event in question, and going to Edit> Travel Time.

Put the watch on a power backup

Draining energy too fast? Swipe up on the home clock screen to open the Control Center. The first icon shows the current battery status.

Press this button to reveal the Power Reserve button.

Unlock your Mac with Apple Watch

If you own a Mac that was built in mid-2013 or later, you can automatically unlock your Mac when it detects that it is near you and using your Apple Watch. To enable the feature, on your Mac, open System

Preferences. Next, select the Security & Privacy option, then the General tab. Finally, select Allow Apple Watch to unlock your Mac's checkbox to enable the feature.

Customize the application dock

Clicking the side button on the Apple Watch will open the app dock, displaying a list of your latest apps by default. What you may not know is that you can customize what appears on your dock, be it your most recent or favorite apps. To change what is shown, head over to the Apple Watch application on your iPhone. After that, select the Dock option. Here, you can choose whether to show recent or favorites. If favorites are selected, you can click the Edit button in the upper right corner and then add or remove the apps you want to view.

Take out the water after swimming

The Apple Watch is water-resistant to 50 meters, but after the dive, you'll still want to use the watch's eject feature to remove water from the built-in speaker. Before jumping in for a swim, swipe up on the Apple Watch face to access Control Center. Then press the Water Eject button; its symbol is a drop of water. Then, as soon as you get out of the water, turn the Digital Crown according to the instructions to remove the water; you may hear beeps during this process.

Use theater mode

You can easily put your watch in theater mode, silence it, and turn off the automatic alarm screen when you need it. To activate theater mode, swipe up from the bottom of the screen while on the watch face. Then select the Theater Mode button (represented by two theater skins). Now your watch will only turn on when you click one of the side buttons. Repeat the procedures above to deactivate this feature.

Listen to music

With an Apple Watch with watchOS 4.1 or higher, you can listen to albums and playlists created on your iPhone, stations on Apple Radio, and any music from Apple Music (if subscribed). You can also listen to audio applications like Spotify, Pandora, and iHeartRadio.

First, set up your headphones, earphones, or speakers via Bluetooth. Open the Apple Music app to browse your library of albums and playlists. From the player, you can pause, resume, skip forward, backward, and control the volume. Apple Radio comes as its own separate app, where you can tune in to Beats 1 and some news and music stations.

To listen to music streaming services such as Spotify, Pandora, and iHeartRadio, you will have to download their apps on your iPhone through the App Store in the Watch app. Each app is slightly different, but the process is the same - just launch the app to access your stations or library. With a paid subscription to a service like Pandora, you can usually do more with your watch, like listening to music offline.

Listen to podcasts

Apple has its own Podcasts application that allows you to download podcasts on the iPhone and listen to them on Apple Watch. And if you have an Apple Watch that supports LTE, you can listen to podcasts without switching to a nearby Wi-Fi network.

Open the Podcasts application on your watch to scroll through the latest available podcasts. You can also access your library to share podcasts or individual episodes. From the podcast player, you can pause, resume, fast forward 30 seconds, go back 15 seconds, change the speed, and change the volume.

You can also play podcasts from your phone using your watch as a controller. And if you're not crazy about Apple's Podcasts app, try some of the third-party apps like Downcast, Overcast, and Pocket Casts.

Talk to someone with Walkie-Talkie

You can talk to another Apple Watch user through the Walkie-Talkie app. Open the application from the home screen (the application that has a black walkie-talkie surrounded by yellow).

Scroll down the contact list and touch a person's name to invite them to speak. Wait for this person to accept your invitation. On the other hand, you can accept an invitation from someone else.

To start a Walkie-Talkie call with a contact, tap the person's name in the app. After the connection is established, press and hold the talk button to talk to the other person. Leave the button to let the other individual respond. Continue the conversation like this, press and hold the Talk button when it is your turn to say something, and then release the button to listen to the other person.

48

Sleep- Page 3
Side button long press — Start of watch.
P P
— How to use apple watch - 33-36

— Watch face changing - P 46

Made in the USA
Monee, IL
29 March 2021